TABLE MANNERS

Table Manners

CATRIONA WRIGHT

THE POETRY IMPRINT AT VÉHICULE PRESS

Published with the generous assistance of The Canada Council for the
Arts and the Canada Book Fund of the Department of Canadian Heritage.

Funded by the Government of Canada
Financé par le gouvernement du Canada | Canadä

SIGNAL EDITIONS EDITOR: CARMINE STARNINO

Cover design: David Drummond
Photo of the author by Emma Dolan
Set in Filosofia and Minion by Simon Garamond
Printed by Marquis Book Printing Inc.

Dépôt légal, Library and Archives Canada and the
Bibliothèque national du Québec, second trimester 2017.

Library and Archives Canada Cataloguing in Publication

Wright, Catriona, 1985-, author
Table manners / Catriona Wright.

Poems.
Issued in print and electronic formats.
ISBN 978-1-55065-467-7 (SOFTCOVER).– ISBN 978-1-55065-474-5 (EPUB)

I. Title.

PS8645.R5188T33 2017   C811'.6   C2016-907360-2
C2016-907361-0

Published by Véhicule Press, Montréal, Québec, Canada
www.vehiculepress.com

Distribution in Canada by LitDistCo
www.litdistco.ca

Distributed in the U.S. by Independent Publishers Group
www.ipgbook.com

Printed in Canada on FSC certified paper.

For my parents

CONTENTS

Three

One

Gastronaut

I would cut off my own thumb for the perfect thimbleful
of wood-ear mushroom and bamboo shoot soup.

My paychecks all go to heirloom parsnips and pickled lamb tongues.
I dream of singed pigs' feet, pearly cartilage and crisp skin.

When Cassie posted those pictures of barbecued tarantulas in Cambodia
I wept with jealousy and rage. It took days and days of foraging
for edible moss just to calm myself enough to sleep.

The candied foie gras is better at Jean Georges than at Mona.
For blocks of congealed chicken blood your best bet is Paz and Petunia.
They churn their own butter.

After I ate my first durian, I didn't brush my teeth for a week.
My breath smelled as though I'd been fellating a corpse.
I coughed on everyone.

I just chose to care about this instead of something else. My life is now
tuned to bone marrow donuts and chef gossip. I'm useless
at any other frequency. At times I'm rancid with resentment,

my body a kingdom of rot. I envy the cavemen their mammoths.
The cannibals their hearts. Lord knows what sumptuous
grubs those elitist toucans gorge themselves on in the Amazon.

White sage and turtle flipper. Turmeric and veal pancreas.
Pine needle and antler velvet. I guess it's as noble and as pointless
and as thrilling and as painful as any other passion.

All my friends are probably off somewhere right now laughing and slurping bird's nest soup while I sit here rearranging items on my bucket list, slipping silkworms into the top slot.

My death row meal is a no-brainer: slow-roasted unicorn haunch and deep-fried fairy wings with chipotle mayo dipping sauce.

Garnish

My earplugs are plush green nubs, Martian thumbs
numbing the blistering blurt of beats that gallop

from the synagogue's stage—the space long ago
deconsecrated, God's clout washed out.

The present is a bland fugue of subterfuge and panic and guilt.
The least I can do is protect my main squeezes, my tympanic

membranes. The DJ's car alarm-inspired aria is translated
into a doorbell ringing again and again: neighbours loaded

with gifts wrapped in cream paper and secured with curly
pastel ribbons, plump, gleaming bouquets accompanied

by heart-shaped cards, casseroles and warm oatmeal cookies
in vintage tins with daisy trims. The gin in my flimsy plastic cup

further softens the clobbering rhythms. My companion—a grim
reprobate who writes clickbait all day—is now a swell date,

his voice a hushed lilting fiddle tune drifting from the moon,
his opinions aligning with mine in lush counterpoint.

I remove the desiccated lime wedge from its forced ledge
and suck, closing my eyes and permitting the poignant nonsense

of my existence to shush my garish dreams. I never eat garnishes.
But when I do I do it slowly, savouring the faded flavours.

Magpie

The woman who eats tar lives next to
The woman who eats detergent who lives next to
The woman who eats dirt

When they carve me open, they'll find bolts, screws
and fine red potter's clay. My baby is half ashes,
half cornstarch, half chalk. In the back garden,
I use both hands to shovel the soil in, tender earthworms
tickling my tonsils, snail shells scraping my tongue.

The woman who eats paint chips lives next to
The woman who eats pebbles who lives next to
The woman who eats wool

I am not one of those monogamists who swoons
imagining the heft of her favourite stationary.
I am as happy wolfing down cream card stock
as I am nibbling gemstone sparkle tissue paper.
Ever since I tore my mouth lock off, I've been binging
like a magpie, on every glint and texture.

The woman who eats mucus lives next to
The woman who eats lipstick who lives next to
The woman who eats bottle caps

Let the tyrants stomp through their kitchens slapping
dazed sous-chefs with steaks. Let them caress
the garlic press and lemon zester. I am not interested
in stoves, those great civilizers. I am not interested in
marinate, broil, bake. Just pluck me a couple of silver
nostril hairs, the coarser the better, and I'll be on my way.

Groceries

I put the edamame in my freezer
with the other edamame.

I ditch the waffles and swirl pudding cups
when I see her standing at the cash.

Her shifts shift with cherry blossoms,
constellations. I can't keep track.

I place the kale in a cold drawer
with the limp kale.

She smiles when she weighs pomegranates,
guides soy milk and flax across a red beep.

The unspit spit shining in her mouth
is a superfood. She sweats agave nectar.

Quinoa with quinoa.
Almonds with almonds.

I want her to imagine me in a tree in tree pose,
filling a gratitude journal with orgasms.

I want it so bad I fill my cart with antioxidants
and silky bowel movements. Nothing that sates.

I sit in the dark and eat boston creams,
their custard a pale mantra.

RibFest

Dibs on the sickest flesh at RibFest.
I'm talking the most murderous
peppercorn rubs, the meanest rum
and Dr. Pepper marinades. I'm talking
pigs with PhDs in tender, cows
who speak fluent mesquite.

That dynamite first taste begot
of ultimatum. I threatened to leave him
if he kept dishing out
buckets of deep-fried gizzards
and gin fizz pitchers every night.

From his side he pulled a hunk of meat.
We stared at it for days, lost.
At last the serpent was brash enough
to take control, grilling it over a fragrant
hellmouth. I can't even describe
the smoky char, the sticky,
caramelized fat, the paradise-fed,
free-range density.

Since then I've wandered through
Texan family reunions and Wisconsin
tailgate cookouts, searched every kalbi stand
in Gangnam, every death metal Finnish food truck.
I've posted on cannibal message boards, stolen
ribs out of a South African baby's hand
and a Siberian mutt's maw. I've followed wafts
into crowded kitchens, spent millions
on cookbooks. Nothing.

Nothing. But tonight, at Muskoka
Ribfest 2014, I'm still hoping
for a meal to match the perfect
fit of those bones curved
to protect my
beloved's
breath.

Mukbang

You sign in to watch her
eat three steaks, a bucket of kimchi, ten carp pastries
filled with custard and red bean paste.

She is size minus ten, but you sign in
to see her eat garlic chicken
with such gusto it lifts loneliness off
your shoulders, loosens your anus.

Your opener is broken, so you stab craters
into a can of tuna, give up,
opt for dill chips and chili dip.

You sign in to see her giggle between spoonfuls
of mayo, to see sauces
accumulate on her teensy chin, to imagine
wiping them off with a spit-damp napkin.

You sign in because your husband is enjoying
the Tuesday night special: beer
after beer after whisky after beer.

Your last non-solo meal was you and your sister
sharing a tub of plain yogurt as skim-milk watery
as a half-hearted subway grope.

The escape key is sluggish, blurred
and sticky with horseradish mustard.

You sign in, you sign in,
you sign in, each screen shining
with her charms, that guileless shoveling:
bibimbap, goulash, shishito burgers.

Her eyes, all whites,
rolled back and watching her own baby
pink brain light up with pleasure.

You sign in to enter the scene, turn off
all the webcams, scrape the plates clean.

To smell the pear detergent's
dim fragrance and to feel
yellow gloves squelch against your fingertips.

To stack rinsed dishes in the rack
as neatly as the unlived lives are folded
in your heart, each one with a sweet splurge
at its core:

banana kick, the perfect kiss,
a daughter to clack utensils with.

Confessions of a Competitive Eater

That it has something to do with amplification seems clear.
Avalanche, trample, the sneaky sublimity of landfills and tulip festivals.

That it has something to do with acceleration seems clear.
Time-lapsed wrinkles, black screens and blank spaces
to signal five years later.

That it is ketchup-tinged burps, Cool Hand Luke swilling pickled eggs,
strawberry milkshake sliding down a throat, the primal thrill
of fill fill fill, a monsoon of Coke.

Something to do with the grotesque,
something bodily.

Jaws trained with regiments of gum.
Gums raw with ghost peppers.

The stomach's greatest gift: to go from heart-
sized to head-sized, hearth, then heavens.

Job Satisfaction

Stylist to star fruit and frozen daiquiris, I understand the right lighting
can detonate salivary glands, expose latent cravings

for mama's ribs or depraved carb binges. Bleaching lackluster cauliflower,
I feel my life force reach dangerously low levels. Then I fluff

a kale ruff and know I am headed straight for purgatory. At least I left
the trenches of plastic cheese, inflated buns and symmetrical sesame seeds,

but these haute couture veggie gigs still leave me empty. If only the sucks
and simps at the food stylist union knew that within their midst

crouched a gastronomic Diane Arbus, dowager of tumourous turnips
and mold-stricken mutton. I haunt fruit fly-infested produce sections

hunting for mangy models. My fridge is a farm team, a start-up
for would-be muses: lapsed hummus and mutated tempeh.

All these stomach-churning stills are still just études for a larger project,
my noir masterpiece with its recurring images of deformity and decay.

The Caper Caper follows two hucksters posing as caper sommeliers
as they swindle their way across the country, promising aspiring caper moguls

a world-recognized rating of !!!! in exchange for a thousand jars.
The final scene is an amateur chef-slash-police chief closing in on them.

We see The Brawns of the operation glance at The Brains with a love as clear
as Just-Married tin cans clattering behind a car. It's evident he wishes

he could pickle that doomed getaway grace. The film ends with a close-up
of a caper, permanently prepubescent, never humiliated

by its petals' imperfect unfurling, its failure to buy a single butterfly a drink.

Bliss Point

Testing can be fun! Just read these tester-monials.
Sami enjoys trying new things.
Lina likes seeing her ideas on the menu.

Testers spend their earnings on lip gloss
or Pepto-Bismol or lettuce.
Some testers send the money home.

We are currently seeking women aged 18-35.
Allergy-free women. Meat-loving women. Guys, babies,
keep an eye out for future opportunities.

Let's begin! Dough: Too crisp? Too soggy? Just right?
Aged cheddar or Swiss? Spicy sauce
or tangy? Two or three pepperonis per slice?

Please no interaction between testers. A certain rigour
dignifies our procedures. The questionnaire is simple
and comprehensive. Here's a glossary of descriptive terms.

Taste-testing requires multidimensional concentration.
Viscosity. Texture. Depth. You'll get the hang of it.
The palate can be trained. Bliss can be optimized.

On a scale of one to ten, how successfully
does the cheeseburger-stuffed crust pizza lessen
the anxiety caused by your social media feeds?

Who do we, the employees of Gastro-Testing Inc.,
remind you of? (Circle all that apply)

a. mother   b. employer   c. lover
d. teacher   e. doctor   f. dealer

When you finished did you feel bloated
or ashamed or proud or as though the surge of grease
had tucked you into a warm, dreamless, padded sleep?

Dietary Restriction

At night I dream of performing polygraph tests
on pomegranates. By day I watch *Tampopo* and think slurp, slurp.

Poco a poco I even begin to feel the miso-loaded mist on my face,
to taste the universe distilled to a rococo so-and-so of noodles and beef.

I can't even seek the brief, shame-inflected relief
of bragging. The whole point of this penitence is to be humble, humbled.

When I visit my ancestor's shrine I find it closed
and encased in a giant yellow dome. No note. Nothing to explain

why my past has been replaced with a Cyclops's lemon drop.
My strength is diminishing fast. I ask a four-year-old girl to eat

a blueberry muffin in front of me and describe the sensation.
When she says yummy and sweet, I slap her,

then fall to my knees and beg forgiveness, kissing
her feet and relishing the coconut sunscreen sting

on my lips. Bit by bit the hunger lessens. Water's subtleties
reveal themselves and I stop picturing the gods

wearing aprons. Of course I slip up from time to time, peruse
the latest reviews of it-joints, read the menus,

all those menacingly homespun promises: *Drones deliver
skewers of pork honk and yolo yam slammers to your table.*

Meals come with sides of triple-fried panopticorn fritters and grits.
After a self-flagellation quickie, the drool dries

and I can return to prayer. As my bones rise to the surface
I receive compliments, envy, concern, then threats

to shove a feeding tube down my throat,
just like they did to my Aunt Gertrude

or was that Eleanor? I don't, can't remember
anymore. Boredom and doubt and history, invasive beetles,

have bored out my family tree, and now the only thing tethering me
to this life is self-discipline, this devotion to hunger. I am still impure

but improving my ability to discern the saints who deserve songs
from those who deserve slaps. I must admit that

if butterscotch rained from the skies, I would join the riots
and streak down the street, syrup,

hot and thick and fawn-coloured, speckling my shoulders.
I would roll in the gutters

until every inch of skin
was covered in stiffening sugar.

Dumpster

I.

Flowers by entrance, flour by
despots' bags of sugar, sugar in hot sauce,
hot sauce in volcanogasm burritos
stacked in freezer, freezer burn
on mango sorbet, sole fillet on ice, icing
three inches thick on every surface.
The only thing rotten
is everything sold here. Everything
glossy and designed to grab a toddler
by the id. The lettuce mister's fine spray,
a tray of fritto misto samples. The yeasty
air fills nostrils, ears swell with schmaltz
and specials. Hands rummage through
rutabagas, palpate avocados. Eyes
ransack nutritional info, compare cuts
of red flesh, hover over fish raised
by thrashing and antibiotics.

II.

Bogus Xanadu of xanthan gum
and mutant grains! I would not let a single
rainbow Chips Ahoy! or briny dill pickle
or cocktail shrimp ring breach my lips
unless it had first passed through the purifying
fires of the dumpster—five star chef, wizard
capable of transforming the too, too processed
into the unsullied fresh. Great liberator
from expiry dates, those false idols of health.
Liberator from plastic bags and points cards
and cash register pings, each red scan
infecting the food with invisible mold.

III.

Divine dumpster, visible to eye and nose,
you have blessed us with your creations
and we come before you with clean bodies and minds
to give thanks for the feasts we forage from you daily,
to sing a praise so loud it can overpower
the garbage truck's oncoming bleeps,
barbarians sparking their blunt axes
against the city gates.

How to Throw a Dinner Party,
or, A Guide to Avant-Garde Table Manners

The Sun King and I, we eat with our hands,
no distance between us and boeuf bourguignon, its cow gut
heat and heft. Thick sauce licked from fingertips.

Whoever requests a fork is deemed a pussy
and thrown downstairs. Oh me and Louis! We go together like meat
and potatoes, like pot and me-time.

We crack eggs on each other. Chives grow from my armpits,
and he grazes until his breath is all onion, and he must ring
for a diminutive minion to scrape his tongue.

Our esteemed guests are cordially invited to sit at the dinner table
and shit. They eat escargot and éclairs in the water closet,
crouched by the emerald-encrusted bidet.

Oh me and Louis! Like a bagel and gelato, a dram of moonshine
and a fiddle. We could write the definitive dinner party listicle:

> 1. No chowder-headed people
> 2. No utensils

Consummate slurpers of consommé, we keep mutton
beneath our fingernails, Dijon splotched
on our cheeks. We reach elbow-deep

into sag paneer, split prawns with our slaps. Here's a tip:
slip LSD from the Loire region in the wine before the salad course.
Of course, never let guests lift a finger.

Let the servants deal with stained lace cuffs, cumin-infused velvets,
mayhem in Art Deco vomitoriums. The servants!
They eat with ivory spoons and sapphire-studded knives

in their dorm rooms, like hillbillies painting the town blah.
They are still operating on the level of cutlery equals class. So passé!
They are as free as spaghetti coiled around steel tines.

Me and Louis? Like tonic and malaria, malaise and nicotine.
He just gets me. When I feel sad he pricks his thumb
and gazpacho pours out. Its spiciness cooled with champagne

soothes me. When we go out for all-you-can-eat sushi, he snaps
our puny chopsticks in half. Nothing can grasp a Kamikaze roll
better than my chomp, each tooth a hostess gift, hand-
pried from a guest's scream.

BBQ

The grapevine is strangling the basil. In the grill coals blink black
then pale grey, shedding the smell of lighter fluid.

All the mint from the balcony bathtub has been juleped.
It is unseasonably warm. We are sensibly drunk.

I am wearing a dress I bought yesterday from my neighbour.
A polyester cosmos of flying saucers and tulips.

We debate day jobs, if they suffocate or inspire.
Dodging our voices, Frank Zappa cackles about rutabagas.

The catfish grows oily and succulent in its foil shroud,
cayenne-dusted whiskers igniting the air.

Two

Origin Story

Some of it was probably cozy and nice. Close to the fire,
silly drunk on sweet fermented plums. Some of it was urgent.

One last romp before the man strapped on his sandals
and dragged his sword into a bloody field. And some quiet,

unbuttoning all those pearl buttons from nape
to feet, folding calf-length velvet breeches before slipping

into cold starch. It's unclear how much cunnilingus went on.
I'm guessing no diamante nipple clamps, but I could be wrong.

Some kinky stuff went down, for sure, maybe involving butter churns.
I don't know. Mammoth tusks? Some people are super brave and creative.

Poems about fleas and dire prophecies and pushy parents
and help with milking and mercy were all possible motives

as were cute overbites and obedience and hunger
and wide birthing hips and relentless seasick nights.

Some of it happened inside a marriage and some outside
and some between enemies in a burning village.

Maybe not all of it was consensual. Let's be honest, history is cruel.
Some women limped out of it, tried to ignore the shame

swelling their bellies. Some women resigned themselves,
just waited for it to end, floating above their bodies.

Some of the women would rather have done it with other women.
Some of the men would rather have been women.

Some couplings were just right, whispering nothings,
mapping mole constellations, all moans and giddy filth.

Back then it couldn't be as clean and deliberate. No thawed vials
of specimen, no donor profiles, no eggs suspended in gel.

Just so many bodies crashing into each other, standing, sitting,
on knees, on beds, with oak bark gnarls pressing

into sweaty backs, with straw in hair, with sand grinding
against hands, with goose down pillowing heads,

the smell of whale oil and opium, of elk velvet, of roast hare,
of piss and mead and beeswax, of coal smoke and manure,

so much skin and so many promises, such love and pain
and contempt and doubt, such hope and duty, all that fucking

creating and creating and creating and creating
you

Instinct

after Delmore Schwartz

I'm not a sloppily stoppered howl,
not a bear in heat trampling ferns for a world of candy
and rage sex. No, I paid someone to siphon the venom
from my ovaries, to destink my pits. The doctor assured me
it was routine surgery, just a few clean snips
to guarantee I won't be tempted to devour
my young. It's over. It's so over. It's been over
seven years since that animal-ectomy.

But I'm still haunted by the beast I might have become.
Sometimes, I dream of potent dung, of crashing
with pure terror through the slippery and scorn-
fueled city. I dream of feathery antennae combing the air
for mates, of tentacles surging from my chest.
I dream I'm a sheep degrading myself for pellets, an all-knees lamb
falling slickly out of me. I awake screaming,
a hand pressed between my legs.

I chase those musky women who rejected the doctor's advice,
those who never tamped down their ribbits
and warbles, those with tails and stench and an endless
amoral hunger, those who will drag their tumourous bodies
into the desert to die. I sit next to them at parties.
I want to feel my skin scraping off
on their rough tongues. I want to suckle, to be stung.
I corner them and jabber praise. They ignore me,
but I can't stop myself.

Date Night #1

> *Oyster foam,*
> *a thousand white gasps.*

Across town in a basement,
my boyfriend holds a mouse
in a soap-foamed bucket
until its debts are paid.

> *Quail egg yolk &*
> *nine grains of pink sea salt.*

We are of an age in an age
of life beyond our means.

What meaning is left
when work is a blister
and food a squeezing of cilantro
on the moon?

> *Lavender-infused cream*
> *solidified tableside in liquid nitrogen.*

Date Night # 2

I.

If disappointment were an organ,
it would look like the severed squirm on my plate.

A Gorgon's lock,
chopped off.

Medusa froze when she saw her reflection.
And I would too if I could see myself
nodding tightly as my date describes the mouth
feel of chanterelles:

their texture, the bliss of walking
on forgiving forest earth in late spring.

I gulp Malbec and reminisce about Paul
the octopus who predicted goals
and penalty kicks, sunlit footballs
curving into nets.

The flounce of his sucker-flexed limbs
descending on the future.

I cut flesh into medals, chew
with eyes closed, praying
those fabled psychic properties
reach my bloodstream.

II.

The weight of the ocean presses
on my eight shoulders.

The weight of ancient oceans
full of indecisive mammals.

The weight of today's oceans
with starfish and blood raining
from above, oil gushing
Bad Thoughts from below.

The weight of future oceans,
glowing and nearly empty,
each lowly mutant

lowing for a mate.

Parties: A Selection

I.

pulled pork   muddled mint
pansexual Prince   all primped
pumping up the crowd

II.

mushrooms in balloons
pills and joints in lacquered bowls
cops cops cops cops cops

III.

themed fun and spiked punch
bedazzled safari coat
breakups imminent

IV.

splattered sangria
candy punched out of a mule
lots of new people!

V.

soulful sing-along
deep fryer   powdered sugar
awkward more awkward

VI.

campfire flattery
who wore the sweater better?
damp grass   leaky shoe

VII.

barbecued tofu
please don't call me a lady
left early   for once

Annual Tea Party

Brass, glass, peaches and cream. Raspberries
shimmer on a tarnished pewter platter.

Great Aunt Hattie pours hard pear cider
into plastic teacups with pink rims.

We stack cucumber sandwiches into Jenga towers.
The words *watercress* and *gooseberry*, dark tickles on the tongue.

Toddlers whirl on the tire swing, conjugating *mourir*.
A smirk of teenagers are in the kitchen memorizing acronyms.

Cousin Beatrice uses rogue strawberries as rouge.
In a dark room her meringue is deflating.

Coconut-heavy Queen Elizabeth cake carved into phalli.
Smoked trout in ragged streaked shreds on crimson foil.

Great Great Aunt Leigh does her party trick: spontaneously combusts.
Wake us up when the extra strong shroom tea has steeped.

Cousin Edna is watching raccoons doing it under a canopy of rhubarb leaves.
She awards them a six for technical and a seven for artistic merit.

It is, we tell Cousin Petunia, just common sense not to eat a pie
baked by your nemesis. That has cannibalism written all over it.

And no duh, Aunt Trish, a scene of two women eating malpeques
with red onion mignonette is a shorthand for lesbian sex.

Cousin Mildred projectile vomits with zero finesse,
as usual, leaves the rest of us to clean up the mess.

We let the vultures peck sweet crumbs out of our hands,
offer the remains to ruthless ant matriarchs.

What a Girl Wants, or, Pledging Allegiance

I escape fig slingers, brie gropers
and dulse munchers only to be brought low
      by marzipanimaniacs, their dainty creations,

miniature cabbages cherubic with grubs,
blind songbirds with silver beaks, skunks
      stinking only of soft almond.

All the loveable scamps of the woodland
and garden, the campy gnomes
      and blushing squash blossoms.

Quail huggers and kale apologists
warn me not to fall for candy's goofy
      charisma, not to confuse gimmicks

for genuine artisanship. I listen and nod
and lift a thimble to reveal the Sydney Opera House,
      a chaser for the Sphinx and Taj Mahal.

Tour

Our riot grrrl group, Gretel Berserk, is on
the growl, a reunion howl hitting every swamp.

Our music is a bolt of raw silk, best suited
for dozens of couture crotchless panties.

Not convinced? You will be. Your life is all galas
and Gossip Girl. A real shabby gabfest. Get ready.

Our backstage rider includes demon tartar, tarantula
caviar and a tarot card reader with a deck full of threats.

The sting is in the riff, kiddies. No smoke machine,
just spliff after spliff until the air is an organza gown.

Correction: we don't glow. We sweat. Enough salt
to preserve four hundred cod for a transatlantic voyage.

Some songs are answers. Some bleed. We turn
down proposals and pee on sticks. Nothing sticks to us.

Skanks and stones. Get up here and say that shit
to our faces. Come on, we triple bitch dare you.

Thought so. We sliced off our right breasts to better aim
our crossbows. We'll give you a demo after the show.

Girl, please! Zeus could come down
as a swan, a computer virus, a tsunami, and still
he would cower before the flounce of our thighs.

BFF

I fed her red gummy bears all through that doubt
bender over the post-Internet album

she'd produced in her bedroom.
I called her songs *Transcendent*

square dances for claymation elf assassins.
I massaged her fingers,

stiff and callused from fiddling knobs.
I was the girl in thrall to her girl

genius, no ambition beyond
buying her tequila shots and feeling blessed.

She hated me for it, of course.
The ephemeralization of my personality,

the way I wanted her to inhale me.
To please her I tried to write poetry, forced whimsy,

to weird it up and be the boss, but it was obvious
I longed to be her chaste wifey, to ball frilly socks.

We filmed a music video in the Mojave,
but I just couldn't writhe fluidly. Coyotes

nipped my ankles, chain mail chafed my nipples.
I ended up on cactus de-fanging duty.

She finally replaced me with a cyborg Dolly Parton,
and every night I imagine the pair of them,

giggling in some after-hours washroom
while they rail angel dust and braid each other's hair.

Fallow Day

Swaddled in my fetid green duvet, I've reached
the heat of a perfect grilled cheese witch,
which is tee-hee because I'm deep in a cold poutine phase—

curds squeaking like Bedlamite mice. 10 am and damn
I've racked up 70 percent of a damsel's
daily recommended sodium.

My laptop, an outsourced organ, is the liveliest thing in bed.
That's what he said. I'm binging on The Bachelor's present tense
eloquence, those blinged out babe sextets.

The ladies erect a cardboard pedestal,
reinforce it with tipsy curses and citrus kisses,
so I can take my place in their pantheon

of Virgo go-getters, panther breathers,
Chardonnay naysayers and kumquats
with squat-firmed flesh.

A jilted sequin getting sparkling wrong,
I rise right out of the rose ceremony, sparking hard,
I settle for a good enough storyline

with a good enough star.

Bridesmaids

The bee balm's spiky fuchsia petals
bring all the butterflies to the yard.

Below the patio table, red toenails, white
Birkenstocks, silver boat shoes, blisters.

Above us, boughs burdened with ripening
pears, squirrels flicking feather-duster tails.

We snack on garlic-doused kale salad, raw
almonds, pale green macarons that taste

of clover. The compost in the corner
is hosting a stink symposium.

The gossip is lazy and vicious. We have
such rich precedents! A girlhood

of sour key-stung lips, scrunchies stacked
ten deep on each wrist. An adolescence

of female-to-female drag—gel-plumped
bras, glittery eyelashes. All sass and disaster,

puking on the principal's loafers. A young
adulthood of mystery bruises, botched dates,

slim paycheques. By the time the sun sets
we have no stories left to tell.

We light the lemon-scented candles.
Lanterns throw warped stars across our throats.

Florist

Dusty miller, thistle, pussy willow,
dried peonies with faded mauve petals,
sage, pink-tinted succulents and sweet peas:

these quiet bouquets, loosely tied with twine,
are my specialty and highly prized
by a certain swathe of women: shy,

prude, prone to quoting poetry,
possessing a prissy reverence
for subtlety. Myself, in short, or what

I once considered myself to be: pastel-
plagued and acutely mute in matters
of sex and humiliation and money.

Across the street another florist's blooms boom,
carnal carnations destined to be tucked behind
flamenco dancers' ears, to absorb sweat

in their flabby petals, or else crude long-stemmed
roses shrouded in baby's breath, prim white dots
as obvious as schoolgirl kilts hiked up.

The customers hail from catholic demographics,
mostly Catholics who saw the *My Big Fat Funeral*
episode that glorified the shop's signature wreaths,

hot pink and orange halos fit for hogs or prom queens.
Tacky, tactless and able to tackle the ugly business
of love and death with blunt sincerity.

I've been practicing in the back with tiger lilies
and hibiscus, with shiny turquoise ribbons
and pinwheels, each spoke a primary colour.

Lineage

If I have a daughter I'll give her a blunt, Teutonic name,
so she can club dumb shit Kindergarteners with it.

I'll take her to the mall and supply the quarters necessary
to blow up space monsters, then watch her engage

with a greasy heap of noodles in the food court.
An easily enraged little sapling,

a reciter of baseball statistics and Rudyard Kipling,
a sporter of shark sweatshirts and smirks,

she'll bring a brutal purity to her role as Clara
in the community Nutcracker production,

cracking the Sugar Plum Fairy's nuts, moshing
with Russians and Arabians. Every pas de chat,

a cha cha paso doble. Every rond de jambe à terre,
a reign of terror. Stomping over the corps'

corpses, she'll eat all the sweetmeats out of traps,
avoiding the sprung snaps, and before the ratty velour

curtains can swish closed, she'll grab a scrap of singed tinsel
off the burning tree, crown herself the new Mouse Queen.

Mother's Day

I.

It hurt, of course. To see them hopping off
to school. To hear the neighbours whisper.
All those theories about too much aspartame
or a one-night stand with the Easter Bunny.

Please don't think me naive.
I know reproduction is a metaphor. Still,
far from the tree
is not far from the orchard.

Nothing could have prepared me to give birth
to nine blue rabbits who all fussed
and turned from my breast,
refused anything but corn syrup.

I wore blue t-shirts, pants, sneakers,
sapphire studs in my ears
and blueberry extravaganza polish on my toes.
I bought a one-size-fits-all bunny ears headband
and matching tail, a poof of cotton accented with tinsel.
I dyed them both fresh indigo.
But they still couldn't see themselves in me.

They couldn't see themselves in anyone.

Some of them tried to pass as normal rabbits.
They got their fur hennaed, adopted
a strictly leaf-based diet, hung around in fields
perfecting their nose twitches.

Some of them clung to their human heritage,
choosing to shave their fur, hide their ears beneath toques,
wear custom-tailored suits, get tattooed, see therapists,
eat caviar and Sour Patch Kids.

Others identified as blue and spent their days
burrowing in piles of Walmart employee smocks
or lying motionless at the bottom of emptied city pools.

A few were proud and would shame
the shame of their brothers and sisters.
They said, "colour-normative worldview"
and "anthropomorphizationism" and "natural ain't natural."
They praised the vibrant hues of their fellow creatures.
      The haute couture iridescence of the peacock!
      The tie-dyed psychedelia of the mantis shrimp!
      The bubblegum-pink dolphins in the Amazon!
      The aquamarine-assed monkeys in the Congo!

II.

Life continued, as it must, past the identity flux
of youth. My brood coped in ordinary ways:
promotions, addictions, marriages, divorces,
mortgages, graduate degrees, gym memberships.

They accepted themselves, had new crises,
reached compromises and sometimes gave up.

One did the circuit of super rabbit obstacle courses
at state fairs. Another toured as a drummer for the band
Dragon Roll Z and the Infinite Wasabi.

One became Distinguished Professor of Animal Studies
by specializing in feco-poetics, another an architect
of luxury hutches in exurban landscapes.

One was butchered, another murdered, another drowned
in a vat of blue curaçao. A heart attack took one,
a tractor accident another.

Through it all they shared one thing:
no offspring.

We'll never know what species the grandkids would have been
or what colour. We'll never know

if grandkids would have made things easier
or if they would have remembered to call today, sent
bouquets of lettuce and lollipops.

III.

I forgive my colony. Just as I hope they forgive me.
It's so easy to let go of all that here, rocking
in my true blue chair, the sky sumptuous in the window.

The fawn I lured inside has latched on strong now.
A steady suckle.
Her eyelashes are so black and luscious.
Just like mine at her age.

Faith

Sunstroked, starstunned, moonstruck.
The universe can have its way with me
as long as it promises the afterlife
is a Terrence Malick movie: shimmery light,
saturated colours, nonsense montages
of bacteria and big bangs.

Wonder is basically a question of scale.
Electrons teleport
in their zigzag orbits, cyclones big enough to swallow
four earths swirl for centuries
on Saturn's uncertain surface.

When the world has reached its wretched
last wheeze, meet me
at the Honey, I Shrunk the Kids Movie Set Adventure
where we will frolic through grief-sized fiberglass
blades of grass and you will bend

on one knee, offer me a single grain of salt,
visible only through microscope,
the last glitter, an antidote
to doubt.

Three

Kiviak, or, Delicacy in Greenland

Caught in long-necked nets, five hundred auks
are stuffed in a seal carcass and buried
under rocks until the nights have gone from jokes
to jabs to death threats and back again.

Flight stilled, eggs denied, the dead birds meditate
in their fatty sepulchre. That airless universe,
a slow cooker. Beaks and bones soften,
feathers melt.

Latitude and chance brought auks and seal
together, joined them in a process more intimate
than digestion. More like gestation.

The birds' bodies, crammed in their surrogate,
are undergoing a drowsy conversion,
gradual then sudden, from corpses
to incubators. The collective gasp
of sugars born again as ethanol.

Exhumed stone by stone, yanked through skin
in a sunlit C-section, the auks spread
their wings as scent. The fermented flesh,
full of vitamins and protein, is a promise
of long life to the bride and groom.

The hearts are slippery and taste like licorice.

Celebrity Chef

He moves through the world with the confidence
        of a matador
                who marinates his sword in barbecue sauce.

In Finland, he eats reindeer steaks and cunt-
        shaped pastries. In Korea,
                he stuffs cabbage into terracotta coffins, buries them.

In Sicily, he is served frozen cuttlefish and scorched risotto.
        He gifts the chef
                ten tar-filled cannoli lavish with icing sugar.

Feijoada. Adobo. Offal links. Sardinas con arroz. Zoodles.
        He is equally happy berating
                philistines and plumping dumplings with grandmas.

He loves his cameraman like mint
        loves lamb. He drinks
                himself into a dungeon every night and every day

he eats his way out.

Hitler's Taste Testers

Me and fourteen other girls. After months, years, of sawdust
and ground acorn coffee, rancid margarine and biscuits
that required a chisel, it almost seemed a gift.

I am disgusted now to admit I was one of his yellow-feathered things,
but there it is. On that first day I shoved fresh vegetables into my mouth.
Asparagus sceptres ennobled with hollandaise, sweet roasted peppers, lettuce,

rice, rich clear broths. No meat or fish. He was a vegetarian
or pretended to be. It's difficult to describe the solemnity of seeing each meal
as your last. We cried with relief when our bowels moved bloodlessly.

But I was hardly a medieval court taster. I never even met him.
We were kept in a separate room, a forced sorority. Forbidden
from seeing our families, we slept on hard beds in a concrete bunker.

At night Anna and Irene analyzed lovers and brothers and other tyrants.
Marlene and Ruth debated belladonna versus arsenic versus hemlock.
Our cycles began to align. We laughed from time to time.

Ingrid did her best Lola-Lola, a blue angel falling
in love again while Ilse giggled, embarrassed, cheeks hot.
Ursula swept our hair into aristocratic knots and swirls.

I can't explain why all fifteen of us had to test his meals
or why we were all women. Helga thought him handsome, deferential
to our fragile bodies. Gertrud punched the wall until her bones went limp.

Equally important was that we be of upstanding German stock
as though we weren't just tasting his food, but digesting it too,
his outsourced intestines.

We were lab rabbits twitching in our cages. Karin wondered if our shared diet
made us more like him or he more like us. Hydrangeas with the same blue hue
dictated by acidic soil. I still can't eat Eintopf or Grießklößchensuppe.

Frieda concocted bold escapes. Eleonore recited verses
from the Book of Job. Lotte found her faith. Sonja lost hers.
We wrote each other's obituaries, full of lewd jokes and accolades.

It went on that way until one night when a soldier who was sweet
on me dragged me from bed and pushed me through an open mouth
in the fence. The Soviets got there soon after

and shot the other fourteen
while the newlyweds dined
on cyanide.

Casseroles, or, Delicacy in Small Town America

Stunned mourners crowd the kitchen, bearing
casseroles dense with salt and fat and childhood
dreams. Green beans suspended in cream
of mushroom soup. Yams smashed and studded
with pastel marshmallows. Pork goulash, meatballs,
cheesy broccoli. Bread crumbs browned, onions
crisp. You eat together in booze-leavened
near silence. Your mind stumbles through half-

remembered rituals. Long ago, in Ireland, a sin eater
unburdened the departed soul by supping on bread
newly risen on the corpse's chest, yeast
replacing those last breaths. Or, no, maybe in Hungary
everyone shared the loaf, perhaps sweetened
with dried plums or ginger, absorbing not the faults
but the social grace or humility of the deceased?

The food wouldn't have mattered to him.
He saw no difference between a hotdog-
stuffed crust pizza and a lobster
and caviar puff and a smoothie rough
with chalky powders. Eating the simplest
way to stay alive, not as it is for you, a spell
summoning scratchy sweaters, the smell of stone
and fire, late November aimlessness—and now

this loss added to that soft blur. Somehow
the day ends. A plate of congealed scoops
wrapped in plastic left at his place. Guests
given souvenirs, shortbread biscuits speckled
with caraway seeds as dark as the beard
trimmings you grumbled over every morning
when you found them scattered in the sink.

Confessions of a Born-Again Cake Boss

Sugarstruck in my fifties, I entered a late cakehood.
Up all night high on fondant fumes and imagined futures,

I started with squares: SpongeBob and monster trucks.
Then I promoted myself to spheres, roulette wheels, stilettos.

Believing myself invincible, I sculpted Tara Lipinski,
her candy skirt uplifted, her lemon legs twisted mid-Salchow.

How I wept when I ate her dull toe pick. Sickened by my hubris,
I began again in earnest: toothbrush, broccoli floret,

garlic press. I untwizzled red liquorice to reproduce the burst
blood vessels in my pug's eyes, left globs in butter frosting

to approximate the cellulite dimpling my neighbour's buttocks.
Inching ever closer to verisimilitude, very soon

I plan to set aside an afternoon for battering
myself, an evening to match the batter

to the queasy chartreuse
of those bruises.

Occult Growers Association Keynote Address, 2075

Forgive me for burning those crops of demons.
I was young. The word 'organic' had divine
authority. Each kale chip a sacrament.
Peer-reviewed articles have since worked
their de-programming magic. Increased yields,
decreased pesticide use. Not to mention the new
redundancy of nitrogen. These creatures are fear-
fertilized, can feed themselves.
It's true their scaly skin and horns all tangled
in stakes is a source of visual pollution.
And yes, the screamed prophecies are harrowing
given the lack of scientific consensus
as to their accuracy. But, I assure you, concerns
about them breeding with bees or weeds or your wife
are entirely unfounded. They're sterile. You won't
be a cuckold raising horned progeny. And think
of the children! All those starving children
plumped and shining with demon vitamins. It's the only
reasonable solution left. Demons and potatoes. Demons on rice.
Demons slow-cooked with fennel and carrots.
Demon burgers, demon smoothies, demon pot pie.
Demon on a stick. Deep-fried demon balls.
So step aside foodies, hippies, anyone
who thinks the word 'natural' has moral weight.
Let those of us who give a shit
feed the world.

Instagram Feed

An apple and a bowl of bran flakes
a day. Too dazed
to type words in any pleasing
order, I arrange
fermented plums and freeze-dried
foie gras dust on an oblong cedar plank.

Marginal calorie calculations
crowd my notebook poems.
The light in my kitchen transforms
curlicues of zucchini into
my corpse's curling nails, still growing.
I blink and all is well again.
My body shrinks.

My belts acquire new holes.
I acquire new likes.
Everyone tells me I look great,
vibrant, so much better.
What did I look like before?
A dizzy energy directs me
to smear chimichurri just so.

At a party a friend drags me to a mirror,
so we can stand side
by side and suck in our stomachs.
She wants to be sure she's still
thinner than me. She is.
I have more followers than her.

I stop writing. My period vanishes.
I use my ink and tampon money
on fairy eggplants and saffron
and photojojo magnetic lenses.

No one intervenes. I spend hours
trying on crop tops and jeans,
strawberry lip gloss and haughty glances,
even though I don't show up
in my own feed. It's all just garnishes
and sauces and sparkling empty
space

Yelp Help

I.

That pub is a bog
standard old man boozer.
The stools are unswivelable.
The music, a classic rock slop
bucket. The taps are busted,
rusted, gunked so bad
the beer tastes like cream
of cauliflower soup. The bartender
is a cad and a bounder,
that is to say, cute.
He has a tattoo on his left shoulder
of me at age two,
my new tiara slipping off
my new head. I beg you,
go anywhere else instead.

II.

That bar is mason jars
and noise. The boys are all feminists
who adore porn and play ukuleles.
The ladies are all burlesque dancers
who love hurling and burly caber tossers.
Everyone knows each other from science
camp or Twitter. One wall is tulip petals,
another bicycle pedals. The shots are ample.
Burps fill the air with dinner samples.
They serve late night liver
and onions, pots of Earl Grey tea.
I've never been there. I'm afraid if I go,
I'll be so comfortable I'll never leave.

III.

That club is a saxophone
solo, the phoned-in sexiness
of men in velvet fedoras and women
in red dresses. You can feel the air
feeling you up. Roses are sold in singles.
Singles mingle with the desperation
of babysitter-bought freedom.
The drinks cost you a firstborn.
The muted horn reminds you
how formal love used
to sound.

IV.

That restaurant is macho chefs
taunting each other and showing off
their knife sets. Joon Min
works in the kitchen. He makes a mean
foie gras and plum crostini,
but whenever I see him I remember
how dumb I was to think
loving canapés
a good enough reason
to marry him.

V.

That diner is a front
for an all-girl gang of giggle dealers. I mean,
the waitresses are dimple models who
serve slices of pie a la mode
with sides of MDMA. A coven
of Jolenes. Each temptress smells like
oven-baked bread and deviant sex.
I would eat only ashes
for the rest of my life if it meant I could lift
one of their eyelashes on my fingertip,
hold it before pursed lips.

VI.

Even the garden salad at this place
could clog a mammoth's arteries.
Paper placemats unfold
into pirate treasure maps. The plates
are plastic. The glasses are plastic.
The cutlery and cheese are plastic.
The plastic is an estrogen hoax.
Waiters there wear nametags and gag
props: Frankenstein bolts,
Flintstone bones, an arrow entering
and exiting at the temples. It is a temple
to bottom feeders and bottomless Cokes,
to our society's craven complacency.
But if you have your heart set, I can
cut you a deal. My mother and I,
we own the place.

Talking to my Father

He slivers the tiniest teensy of apple torte.
I've never rationed anything in my life.
My blood, all sweet dumdums and temper tantrums.

He writes funny, sad, umami emails
just for me. I write schlock and smarm
and post it, wait for the world's praise.

His bookcases are full of gilt and canon.
Cognac swirls in a big-bellied glass.
Hot takes blur behind my thin vape.

All winks and nudges, he tells me careers exist
for whistling. I extinguish thirty candles, wishing
for a job that doesn't itch as much.

He trusts human ingenuity and low-fat diets.
When he was a child, the planet wasn't aging
so fast. The almonds I adore were born in thirst.

The sutures have healed in his chest.
My heart is still planning her debut revolt.
Maybe if I could just step into a wormhole

and come out in the seventies, we could sit
and share a cheese and leek strudel, listen
to songs about a world we both believe in.

Home Body

You can take me anywhere. I can strip
the willow & sing La Marseillaise.
I can smile & lie & deconstruct The Wall.

But I'd rather be reclined on flannel,
conducting a bonbon orgy.
Om nom nom, a life organized

around feedings & groomings.
I summer in e.e. cummings
& winter in goose down duvet.

I can spend a whole day piping
garlands of mini buttercream rosettes
on a million-layer cake,

anything to stop the shakes.
Every whim can be delivered
these days, even clay face masks

& purses shaped like praying
mantises. I wink at myself
in the smudged mirror & practice

accepting compliments.
People out there smell
of *excuse me* & microprocessors.

They're all in cahoots with bots
& bitumen spills & just
aimless bitchiness.

And there are so many.
They ask me & they ask me
to speak up. Enough!

Much safer to read Plath
in the tub, a beehive of suds
fizzing on my head.

Honeymoon

Iceland's July is all days. The sky never dims
below a milky grey. Days of blue
mussels served on slabs of polished slate, tourist-
tiny rotten shark cubes chased with birch sap cocktails.

In wool sweaters, black sand grouting our boot soles,
we leave our rented apartment for the grocery store.
Slopes and winking dots float above vowels, an accessorized
and uncanny alphabet. Bog-brown lamb's heads
wrapped in cellophane, speckled puffin eggs, cod
livers in tins, thin dried puddles of fish, like dehydrated ghosts.

Strolling through the aisles, we adjust. The carts smaller,
the bottles of Coke smaller, but the same familiar blast
of rotisserie chicken, familiar fluorescent lights
blanching skin, familiar sugars and fats
stacked by the cash, goading our impulse control.

We bicker our favourite bicker over the relative
nutritional merits of broccoli versus kale versus bean sprout,
agree we both married an idiot, then fill our basket
with farfalle, leeks, smoked salmon, passive soft
cheese. Our food beeps. We pay and leave.

The air tastes sulfurous, the island too young to insulate
all that heat we know, but often forget, is boiling
beneath our feet. We discuss our plans for the evening:
the food, the dishes, and then Dream Wife,
an all-girl band we will scream along to for the next decade.

On Not Letting Myself Go

My caretaker, bone shimmer
brightening her tear ducts,
barbed wire tattoos
tenderizing her arms, works
the shampoo into a tight
prismatic lather, thumbs pressing
my scalp, each finger
a search party member
parsing damp woods
for missing girls. A chasm
opens in my chest. I clamp
onto armrests to prevent
myself from floating, bumping
into the champagne stucco
ceiling. What is her name again?
This black vinyl cape crinkles
with each twitch. Above me
scissors chirp and dart. On my hair
she dumps celestial powders,
putties. I can smell her
sweat sweetened with a lemon
melon undertone. Deodorant
or perfume or memory?
Limp strands are yanked
around boar bristles, plumped
under hair dryer blasts
as brutal as a daughter's
exasperated sighs. My neck
creaks, my toes throb, waking
up. Is she, like me, the type
who only eats the pink trench
from tubs of harlequin

ice cream? She soaks my nails
in a shallow bowl full of citrusy
chemicals, files them
into crescents a forensic expert
would swoon to swab
beneath. White lilies glisten
on my pinkies. Safely
embalmed, a body again,
I reach into my purse, a whirlpool
of lipstick-blotted tissues, smeary
goodbye kisses, and extract
enough wrinkled tens.

Crone

I'll wear asymmetrical, gem-toned muumuus
and thick cords adorned with ceramic speculum pendants.

Dependant-free, just me and my harpy-self, burlap sack
bursting with razor-lanced caramels and poisoned ring pops.

I'll learn ballet through spells, pas de chat my way to the local cafe
where I'll order a carafe of moonshine and a charcuterie plate.

While stuffing my face with fat-spackled pate and pickled cobra eggs,
I'll riff with my scruffy waiter about mystics. Kabbalah, blah, blah…

On lazy Sundays I'll shoplift dildos, take blimps for joyrides, juice kale
and the fabbest new steroids, splurging on extra for my Aqua Fit buddies.

By moonlight I'll paint cubist portraits of prolific succubi,
turpentine fumes doing the mess around with my brush strokes.

In those magic hag years I'll be so freaky blissed
I'll cease to exist.

Lullaby

Twenty suns set
in black and white
on the wall of monitors.

This shelter sure is swanky,
all Motown vinyls
and freeze-dried meats.

I swing my gas mask nozzle
back and forth, and stamp
my feet, an elephant
in the throes of grief.

The thread count of the sheets
is infinity times infinity
plus one.

The world has gone on
long enough.
Now it's time to sleep.

NOTES

"Magpie" is dedicated to the character Rebeca Buendía, an orphan who finds comfort by eating earth and whitewash, from Gabriel García Márquez's *One Hundred Years of Solitude.*

"Mukbang" is inspired by popular live-streaming webcasts in South Korea in which hosts enthusiastically consume enormous meals while the audience provides feedback via chat.

"Bliss Point" is indebted to Michael Moss' *Salt Sugar Fat: How the Food Giants Hooked Us* (2013, Random House).

In "How to Throw a Dinner Party, or, A Guide to Avant-Garde Table Manners" the term "chowder-headed" is stolen from Herman Melville's *Moby-Dick.*

In "BFF" the italicized lines are slightly altered versions of things Grimes (Claire Elise Boucher) wrote on her Tumblr in 2014.

"Mother's Day" is dedicated to Mary Toft, who convinced doctors in 1726 that she had given birth to a litter of rabbits. The poem also draws from Andrew Solomon's *Far from the Tree: Parents, Children and the Search for Identity* (2012, Scribner).

"Kiviak, or, Delicacy in Greenland" is indebted to episode three of BBC's *Human Planet* documentary series.

"Hitler's Taste Testers" is dedicated to Margot Woelk, the only surviving food tester. She began to speak publicly about her experience in 2013. The names of the fourteen other taste testers have been fictionalized in this poem.

"Casseroles, or, Delicacy in Small Town America" is inspired by the episode "Funeral Food" from the podcast *A Taste of the Past,* hosted by Linda Pelaccio.

ACKNOWLEDGEMENTS

Poems from this collection have previously appeared in *Lemon Hound*, *Prism International*, *The Rusty Toque*, *Echolocation*, *Room Magazine*, *The Humber Literary Review*, *Arc Poetry Magazine*, *Prairie Fire*, *The City Series: Toronto* (Frog Hollow Press), and *Best Canadian Poetry in English 2015* (Tightrope). Thank you to all the editors.

"Confessions of a Competitive Eater" & "Gastronaut" & "Magpie" won the 2014 *Matrix Magazine* LitPop Award (judged by Matthew Zapruder)

"Kiviak" was awarded an honourable mention in the 2014 Bliss Carman Poetry Award (judged by Sue Goyette)

"Tour" was a finalist for the 2014 *Walrus* Poetry Prize

"BBQ" was a finalist for the 2014 National Magazine Award

"Lineage" was shortlisted for the 2015 *Prism* International Contest

"Hitler's Taste Testers" was shortlisted for the 2016 *Arc* Poem of the Year Award

Thank you to the Ontario Arts Council for support through the Writers' Work in Progress and Writers' Reserve programs. Thank you to Carmine Starnino for the thoughtful edits and to David Drummond for the gorgeous cover.

Thank you to the many people who first read these poems, especially Laura Clarke, Michael Prior, Vincent Colistro, Michelle Brown, Phoebe Wang, Bardia Sinaee, Matt Loney, Andy Verboom, Daniel Renton, and Jess Taylor.

Thank you to all my wonderful friends for your encouragement and support. Thank you to Myra Bloom for making me believe I could write poems.

Thank you to my family, who taught me to love, fear, and respect food. Our dinner table conversations about cannibalism and Ritz mock apple pie inspired this book.

Finally, biggest thank you to Ted Nolan for your patience, your intelligence, and your gumbo.

Signal
EDITIONS

Carmine Starnino, Editor
Michael Harris, Founding Editor